Hello, America!

Statue of Liberty

by R.J. Bailey

Bullfrog
Books

Ideas for Parents and Teachers

Bullfrog Books let children practice reading informational text at the earliest reading levels. Repetition, familiar words, and photo labels support early readers.

Before Reading

- Discuss the cover photo. What does it tell them?
- Look at the picture glossary together. Read and discuss the words.

Read the Book

- "Walk" through the book and look at the photos. Let the child ask questions. Point out the photo labels.
- Read the book to the child, or have him or her read independently.

After Reading

- Prompt the child to think more. Ask: Have you ever been to the Statue of Liberty? Did you go inside the statue?

Bullfrog Books are published by Jump!
5357 Penn Avenue South
Minneapolis, MN 55419
www.jumplibrary.com

Library of Congress Cataloging-in-Publication Data

Names: Bailey, R. J., author.
Title: Statue of Liberty / by R.J. Bailey.
Description: Minneapolis, MN: Jump!, Inc., 2016.
Series: Hello, America! | "Bullfrog Books."
Includes index. | Audience: Age 5-8.
Audience: Grades K-3.
Identifiers: LCCN 2016010949 (print)
LCCN 2016012729 (ebook)
ISBN 9781620313510 (hard cover: alk. paper)
ISBN 9781624963988 (e-book)
Subjects: LCSH: Statue of Liberty (New York, N.Y.)—Juvenile literature. | New York (N.Y.)—Buildings, structures, etc.—Juvenile literature.
Classification: LCC F128.64.L6 B35 2016 (print)
LCC F128.64.L6 (ebook) | DDC 974.7/1—dc23
LC record available at http://lccn.loc.gov/2016010949

Editor: Kirsten Chang
Series Designer: Ellen Huber
Book Designer: Molly Ballanger
Photo Researcher: Kirsten Chang

Photo Credits: Age Fotostock, 3, 18; Alamy, 9, 20–21; Corbis, 16; Getty, 4, 14–15, 17, 18–19; Lee Snider Photo Images/Shutterstock.com, 23bl; Shutterstock, cover, 1, 5, 6–7, 8, 12–13, 20–21, 22, 23tl, 23tr, 24; Superstock, 10–11, 23br; Thinkstock, 12–13.

Printed in the United States of America at Corporate Graphics in North Mankato, Minnesota.

Table of Contents

Lady of Light

There she is! Who?

The Statue of Liberty.

She is on an island.

It is in New York Harbor.

harbor

island

Wow! She is tall.

How tall?

She is 151 feet
(46 meters)!

8

Who made her?

Builders in France.

9

It was 1886.

She was a gift
to America.

She is a symbol
of freedom.

She holds a book.

What is written on it?

A date.

July 4, 1776.

That's America's birthday!

13

She has a torch.

It is lit.

She holds it high.

She wears a crown.
It has spikes. How many?
Seven.

spikes

We can go inside.

17

Let's go up.

Wow! There are
lots of stairs.

Look!
We can see far.

We love Lady Liberty!

Lady Liberty Up Close

spikes
The Statue of Liberty's crown has seven spikes. They are meant to be a halo, a circle of light used to symbolize perfection.

torch
The flames of the torch are gold-plated, which makes it appear to be lit.

crown
There are 25 windows in the Statue of Liberty's crown.

book
The date on the front of the book is the day the American colonists declared themselves a separate country independent of British rule.

Picture Glossary

France
A country
in Europe.

statue
A likeness
(as of a person)
sculpted in a
solid substance.

harbor
A place on the
coast where
boats and ships
can enter.

symbol
A design, figure,
or object that
represents
something else.

Index

To Learn More

Learning more is as easy as 1, 2, 3.

1) Go to www.factsurfer.com

2) Enter "StatueofLiberty" into the search box.

3) Click the "Surf" button to see a list of websites.

With factsurfer.com, finding more information is just a click away.